To Alex Laing (1955-1988)

LIVERPOOL

Images of a great seaport

Merseyside Development Corporation is pleased
to sponsor this attractive publication. It shows
superbly the heritage of Liverpool's past – with
its magnificent Victorian and Georgian buildings
– together with the legacy being created in the
present by the regeneration of Merseyside.
The Development Corporation is proud to play
a major part with a programme of sensitive
refurbishment and construction, in conjunction
with other agencies on Merseyside.

"Liverpool: Images Of A Great Seaport" has an
important role in the task of displaying the genuine
advantages of the area as an attractive place in
which to live, work and play.

Sir Desmond Pitcher
Chairman, Merseyside Development Corporation

TEXT
Written by Deirdre Morley

DESIGN
Designed by Corporate Culture Limited, Liverpool

PHOTOGRAPHY
Alex Laing was commissioned to take photographs for this book and most of the images
reproduced here are his work. Following his untimely death, Peter Whitfield and Peter Hagerty
completed the book, with additional support from Stephen Brock, Ron Davies, Steve Hale, Ron
Jones, Christian Smith, David Williams and Guy Woodland. Cover photographs by Ron Davies

PRODUCTION
Typesetting output by P's & Q's, Liverpool
Origination by Creation Graphics, Birkenhead

Published in 1992 by
The Bluecoat Press, Bluecoat Chambers, School Lane, Liverpool

ISBN 1 872568 00 9 Liverpool

INTRODUCTION

Liverpool is a city that should be approached from the water. As you cross the great, grey width of the River Mersey to the towers on the metropolitan shore, you begin to get the feel of the place and a sense of what has made it.

Like Venice, it is wedded to the sea. Sea trade brought Liverpool vast riches and built the city that we see today. The process was not gradual but sudden and dramatic. In the second half of the eighteenth century, Liverpool rose with a rush. In less than a generation, the population doubled; the Mersey teemed with ships, streets spread over the fields and travellers came from far and wide to witness the unprecedented phenomenon. Liverpool was a wonder. Within the space of a lifetime, an obscure town, on the banks of a quiet river, had been transformed into the capital of a seaborne commerce that encompassed the world.

The key to this dazzling success lay in a unique conjunction of enterprise and opportunity. For hundreds of years, England's chief trading interests had been centred in Europe, far from the north-west coast and, although King John had created Liverpool a borough in 1207, very little development followed. However, with the eighteenth century came the industrial revolution and the opening up of America. Against this background, Liverpool's geographical position presented remarkable advantages. Built at the estuary of the Mersey and offering a natural harbour, the town looked outward to the new world and inland to some of the richest coalfields and iron ore mines in the country. All was set for an expanding economy and the townsmen of Liverpool seized their opportunity with such vigour and efficiency that, within a very short time, the port's pre-eminence was assured.

In 1710, the Corporation of Liverpool began building the world's first commercial wet dock in what is now Canning Place. By the end of the eighteenth century, Liverpool possessed a complete system. None of its rivals had built more than a single dock. In fact, trade was so brisk in the town that dock building could scarcely keep pace. In particular, the port was growing fat on the nefarious three-cornered trade: weapons, salt and trinkets to Africa; slaves to the Americas; rum, sugar, tobacco on the homeward run.

Legend has it that slaves were regularly chained to the walls of the Goree Piazzas, a large warehouse complex that once stood behind the offices of the Mersey Docks and Harbour Company. These buildings were certainly associated with the trade for they were named 'Goree' after a slaving entrepot in the Cape Verde Islands but, in fact, there was

never any systematic importation of slaves to England. The essential feature of the vile triangular trade was that its merchant impressarios reaped their huge profits without ever having to see their cargoes of human flesh.

In 1807, Parliament abolished slavery and Liverpool's MP, William Roscoe, both spoke and voted for the act which ended the trade. He returned home to a violent reception, since most of the townspeople were convinced abolition would mean their ruin. Instead, Liverpool became the boomtown of the nineteenth century. Immense warehouses - Britain's biggest - became a feature of the town (and a sure indication of its wealth). Steel and steam revolutionised shipping, while the railways - the Liverpool and Manchester Railway opened in 1830 - gave the town superb communications on land. Talent flocked in, fortunes were made, more docks were built and the port trade grew even faster. In 1825, the tonnage into the port was 1.2 million; by 1865, 4.7 million and by 1900, when Liverpool owned a seventh of the total registered shipping of the world, the tonnage had risen to 12.4 million.

The expansion in trade was matched by an expansion in population. By the time Liverpool's importance was officially recognised by the granting of city status in 1880, the population had reached over half a million - more than twelve times its size a hundred years before. Among the throng of immigrants, Irish, Welsh and Scottish figured prominently. Later, they were joined by Africans, West Indians, Chinese and people of many other nations. Liverpool took on a cosmopolitan character.

But as thousands settled, thousands more simply passed through, for Liverpool was Europe's main gateway to America. In 1840, the Cunard Company inaugurated a regular fortnightly service to New York aboard the steamship liner Britannia. Other famous lines - the Blue Funnel, the White Star - followed. The age of the passenger liner had begun, with Liverpool at its centre.

Innovation was the business of this bold young city. The past did not signify. Only the emblematic Liver Bird, derived from the Eagle of St John

Perch Rock Fort and Lighthouse at the mouth of the Mersey

on the royal letters patent of 1207, survived as a link with Liverpool's medieval origins. Even the mighty castle disappeared. Begun not long after the Norman conquest, it withstood three sieges during the civil war, only to be swept aside in the eighteenth century by a citizenry with its eye fixed firmly on the future. As late as the first half of the twentieth century, the city seemed too new, too brash, to have a heritage of historic importance.

How differently we see things now! For, vividly reflected in the streets and buildings of Liverpool, is the story of the greatest social and economic transformation that history has recorded - the industrial revolution. It began in Britain and Liverpool was its frontier town. In the 1980s, attention turned to the conservation of this unique legacy, spearheaded by the Merseyside Development Corporation, whose farsighted policies, together with those of Liverpool City Council are creating an exciting future for Liverpool as a major centre of tourism.

Nowhere is it more spectacularly demonstrated than on the waterfront. Here, the magnificent Albert Dock - the first enclosed, incombustible dock warehouse system in the world - has been restored and sensitively redeveloped with shopping and leisure facilities, office and residential accommodation. It also houses a superbly sited Maritime Museum and the Liverpool Tate Gallery, offering its dazzling collection of modern art.

Once again, people are discovering Liverpool. In the past they came as fortune-hunters or refugees; today they come as visitors, attracted by the city's unique heritage of history, culture and architectural grandeur. As Liverpool's resurgence progresses into the 1990's, more and more is being rediscovered, appreciated, conserved and developed.

This book sets out to celebrate the Liverpool of today in relation to its rich and historic past. It is not a guidebook as such but rather an evocation of the city and the features that make it unique.

THE RIVER

'The mouth of the Mersey is armed with lighthouses, landmarks, beacons, telegraph stations and private signal poles, as a mouth with teeth', wrote a German visitor of 1842, JG Kohl.

Now, as ships enter the estuary, their view to port is dominated by cranes, an army of them, standing like sentinels from Seaforth Dock to Liverpool Pier Head. These are the north docks, the working docks, handling timber, grain, meat and general cargo on a vast scale.

To starboard, the sights are altogether more unexpected. A massive red sandstone fortress rears up out of the sea. Its batters, towers and parapet suggest a medieval construction but Perch Rock Battery is, in fact, a product of the Napoleonic Wars. Built in 1827 (long after hostilities had ceased), it once trained 18 guns onto the estuary in defence of the port of Liverpool. Today it houses a museum and, at low tide, visitors can walk across a man-made causeway and enter through the fort's imposing Tuscan gateway.

A little to one side stands the Fort's companion piece, the Rock Lighthouse. Built of Anglesey granite, each stone has been dovetailed into the next and the whole weather proofed with a coating of pozzoulana, a cement of volcanic origin, imported from Italy, which possesses a property ideal for this kind of purpose - it hardens under water. The lighthouse, completed in 1830, greatly impressed Herr Kohl on his visit twelve years later. He thought it 'the most important, the most solid and the handsomest' of its kind.

Behind it, on a succession of lofty ridges, rise the ornamental villas of New Brighton. Executed in a kind of wedding cake architecture, their white and vanilla stuccoed facades, punctuated with the cast-iron tracery of balconies and verandahs, make a delightful backdrop to the river. The whole town was conceived in the 1830s as a fashionable watering place by eminent Liverpool entrepreneur, James Atherton. In a few years, he had transformed what was then 'a mere heap of sand-hills' into a highly desirable marine residence.
The opening of a railway tunnel under the Mersey, in 1886, provided an all-weather connection with Liverpool that quickly made New Brighton a popular resort for day-trippers.

Before the coming of the railway, the journey had to be made by boat and, all along the south shore of the broad river, ferries plied back and forth. Ferries have crossed the Mersey for hundreds of years. They were already well established when King Edward III granted the Benedictine monks of Birkenhead Priory the legal right of ferry to Liverpool in 1330.

The Royal Charter which granted that right 'forever' to them and their successors, still protects the ferry service. An act of Parliament is needed to revoke it.

The original Monks' Ferry has gone (but the ruined Priory remains and can

be visited). The modern ferryboats accommodate some 1200 people and cross from two points: Woodside in Birkenhead and Seacombe in Wallasey.

There is no more exciting or evocative way to enter Liverpool than by ferryboat. Facing a great river with a tidal range of over 30 feet, the ferries make a fast crossing yet, no matter how many time you make the trip, there is still a sense of adventure to be had in this short voyage 'over the water', as the local phrase has it.

Liverpool's famous waterfront derives its distinctive quality from three buildings at its centre; the Royal Liver Building, the Cunard Building and the headquarters of the Mersey Docks and Harbour Company. Monumental and magnificent, they confront the river with all the dignity and imperial splendour of Edwardian enterprise.

The Liver Building is probably Liverpool's best known landmark. Designed with outstanding originality and power by W Aubrey Thomas and erected between 1908 and 1911, it continued the tradition of architectural innovation for which the city had become famous in the previous century. Although one cannot tell from the outside, the Liver's massive walls of glittering granite conceal a steel and concrete framework - one of the world's earliest expressions of this form of multi-storey construction. It is now Grade 1 listed.

Crowning the eleven storeys are two clock towers (their dials larger than those of Big Ben) and these are surrounded by cupolas on which perch the city's fabled Liver Birds.

With its flamboyant architectural features, the Liver Building stands in marked contrasts to its neighbour, the Cunard. Built during the First World War for the great shipping line after which it is named, the mood of the Cunard Building is more restrained but no less mighty.

Its grandeur reflects the fact that Liverpool was the Cunard Line's terminus from 1840 until 1919. It was from this port that the company's first transatlantic passenger vessel, the Royal Mail Steamship, Britannia, sailed in July 1840, soon to be joined in regular crossings by sister ships which were judged by Herr Kohl to be 'specimens of architecture quite as wonderful as many a temple or custom house'.

The massive granite facade of the Royal Liver Building

The Port of Liverpool Buildings, headquarters of the Mersey Docks and Harbour Company

When it came to choosing a design for their headquarters, Cunard commissioned Willink and Thicknesse to build in the style of a sixteenth century Italian Palazzo, with Greek Revival detail. Its simple square shape, heavily rusticated Portland stone and fine proportion creates an air of immense solidity and austere elegance.

The third building on the spacious Pier Head plateau is far from austere. The offices of the Mersey Docks and Harbour Company were completed in 1907 to a design of great pomp and circumstance by Arnold Thornley. They combine the features of a grand Renaissance palace with those of a great church by Wren or Bernini. The ecclesiastical impression is largely created by a central classical dome, not unlike that of St Paul's Cathedral in London. Inside this impressive structure of Portland stone, an octagonal hall rises up 220 feet to the dome with arched galleries running round it at four levels.

It is fitting that this impressive trio

of buildings should form the focal point of Liverpool's waterfront for, between them, they reflect the city's three major commercial interests from which her vast riches derived: the port, shipping and insurance. And yet, these buildings are relative newcomers on the city-skyline.

Throughout the first one hundred and fifty great trading years, it was dominated by far less sophisticated, though no less potent symbols of wealth - warehouses.

For mile upon mile, they stretched along the shore, plain and apparently uniform, sombre and strong, fortresses of tangible wealth. They harboured fortunes in commodities: sugar and rum from the West Indies; grain, cotton and tobacco from America; cocoa and ivory from West Africa, forming a square of rich, russet brick around the dark still waters of the dock.

When the Prince Consort came, in 1846, to open this magnificent complex which bears his name, he

silks from the Far East; rice, tea and jute from India, wines from the Mediterranean.

Look south from the Pier Head and you can still see what is perhaps the finest example of this architectural form - the mighty Albert Dock.

It is a monumental construction: five massive blocks, each five storeys high,

remarked: 'I have heard of the greatness in Liverpool, but the reality far surpasses the expectation . . .' He was bearing witness to more than the successful conclusion of yet another vast enterprise in the second city of the British Empire. The Albert Dock marked an historic step forward, not only for the port of Liverpool but for dock design throughout the world.

Here, warehouses were designed as an integral part of the scheme. Until the Albert Dock was built, goods arriving in Liverpool by ship were simply unloaded straight on to the quayside and, if need be, stored there temporarily in sheds, until they could be reloaded on to carts (pulled by a special breed of giant dock horse). Then they were hauled off to privately owned warehouses where they had to be unloaded a second time. The great advantage of an enclosed dock system, like the Albert, built with warehouses as an integral part of the design, is that goods can be unloaded directly into those warehouses. This reduces the risk of damage by repeated handling and the risk of loss by pilfering.

Liverpool Corporation had investigated the possibility of an enclosed system of public warehouses as early as 1803 but private warehouse owners, protecting their vested interests, succeeded in delaying the development for more than 30 years. As a result,

(Above) The monumental five-storey Albert Dock warehouses
(Left) Octagonal Watchman's Hut, Canning Half-Tide Dock

St Katherine's Dock, London was the first to be built. However, a later start allowed Liverpool to improve on the original. Crane arches were incorporated in the Albert warehouses to enhance cargo handling - a big step forward - and hydraulic machinery was introduced.

Above all, the entire complex was fireproof: the construction is wood-free, being entirely of brick and iron.

This was a vital advance because, next to drowning, fire was the commonest tragedy in the port, as any random examination of the city annals will show. For example, the year the 'fire police' was established - 1834 - began with a windmill burning down. On 17th January, the City of Dublin Company's Warehouse, Clarence Dock, shared the same fate (loss £2000). The year ended thus: 'October 16th a fire took place in

Lancelot's Hey at Dover Warehouses when property to a great extent was destroyed. December 2nd, the Castle Mills, Chaucer Street were burned down; on the 27th, Messrs Foster and Stewart's, builders, extensive workshops were also destroyed..' 1835 began in similar fashion with the workshop of Messrs Foster and Griffin burning down on 31st January.

The mastermind of the Albert Dock

Hartley's precision can be seen in his masterly handling of stonework throughout Albert Dock

was Jesse Hartley and masterful is unquestionably the epithet that describes him. He was a Yorkshireman, born in Pontefract in 1780, a bridgemaster who, when he was appointed Dock Engineer to the Port of Liverpool in 1824, had no direct experience of dock construction. Nevertheless, in the next 36 years, he proved to have formidable talents, constructing or altering every dock in the city with outstanding proficiency. He added 140 acres of wet docks and 10 miles of quay space, working in the most economical and efficient manner, paying meticulous attention to detail and insisting on the highest quality of workmanship, of composition and finish. His agreement with contractors for the Albert Dock, for example, called for specified bricks and was punctuated by severe penalty clauses. The Cyclopean masonry courses of each dock basin - which present a pleasant crazy-paving effect to the eye - were minutely planned. Each stone was recorded on a diagram by colour-coding, to show when and by which contractor it was laid. Monthly running totals were also recorded. Mr Hartley liked a proper job.

His innovations were legion. One
example is in his use of galvanised
iron plates on the roofs of the Albert
warehouses. Although iron plates had
been used before in roof construction,
he introduced a novel feature, the
plates are riveted together to form one
of the earliest instances of a curved,
stressed skin construction. Ever
active, he also introduced hydraulic
power and railways onto the docks,
purchased a quarry for materials as a
cost-cutting measure and constructed
a fleet of dock workboats for similar
reasons of efficiency and self-
sufficiency. He also began the
practice of making an annual report.

Hartley was described by a
contemporary, the Liverpool historian
Sir James Picton, like this: 'large build
and powerful frame, rough in manner
and occasionally rude, using
expletives which the angel of mercy
would not like to record; sometimes
capricious and tyrannical, but
occasionally where he was attached, a
firm and unswerving friend.
Professionally he had grand ideas and
carried them into execution with a
strength, solidity and skill which have
never been exceeded.'

*Further examples of Hartley's
skilful handling of iron and stone*

Those professional qualities are
nowhere better demonstrated than in
the Albert Dock, now superbly
restored and imaginatively
redeveloped with shops, restaurants,
leisure attractions and business
accommodation. But the biggest

attraction of all remains the delightful ambience of the Albert Dock itself. Picton thought it lacked beauty but to the modern eye this judgement seems quite wrong. The design is one of uncompromising and elegant simplicity, carefully proportioned, strongly stated and executed in materials that impart a warmth to the whole. The four upper floors of the warehouses are carried on a fine colonnade of massive cast iron Doric columns which stand on the very edge of the quayside. At intervals, the columns are more widely spaced and here wide, shallow arches spring between them, lending a note of grace to the facade. These waterside arcades, once wholly practical in function, can now be enjoyed at leisure. One of the most satisfying pleasures of the Albert Dock is to walk along the quayside, under Hartley's generously proportioned arches, perhaps lean against a vast terracotta-coloured column and simply watch the sheltered waters gleam in the sunshine.

A few short years ago this beautiful complex stood derelict. Then, in 1981, the Merseyside Development Corporation was created by act of Parliament and given the immense task of regenerating 865 acres of dockland on both sides of the River Mersey. The Albert Dock - the largest group of Grade I listed buildings in the country - required extensive work including dredging of the dock itself and repair of extensive war damage. The result is a triumph. Moreover, Hartley's buildings have proved eminently adaptable to a wide variety of uses: a major modern art gallery, housing, television studios, offices, shops and a maritime museum are all accommodated.

The Tate Gallery ingeniously uses the open warehouse space to present contemporary art on a dramatic and accessible scale

As a setting for the superb modern art collection of the Tate Gallery in Liverpool, the Albert Dock seems an ideal choice. In the hands of architect James Stirling (who was educated locally at Quarry Bank School and Liverpool University School of Architecture), Hartley's masterpiece has adapted to this new use particularly well.

Granada Television has converted the former Dock Traffic Office into a prestigious centre for their news operation. It is built in the form of a classical temple but with the fascinating feature that the entire portico is cast in iron. The shafts of those four great columns (almost 18 feet in height) are iron (cast in two halves and welded along their length) - as are the architrave, frieze and cornice. The building was designed by Philip Hardwick (of Katherine Dock and Euston Arch fame) in consultation with Hartley who added the upper storey.

The cast-iron portico of Philip Hardwick's Dock Traffic Office

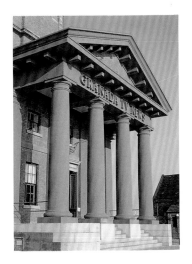

To the rear of Granada TV News stands the main building of the Merseyside Maritime Museum in one of five Albert Dock warehouses. Again, it has converted superbly to its new function and, again, it is hard to imagine a better setting for a venture of this sort: behind it, the broad expanse of the river; before it, the very heart of Liverpool's historic dockland.

The museum actually occupies the Canning Docks, which were built for sailing vessels in the early years of the 19th century. These docks have been superbly restored, along with their handsome quayside buildings and, once again, ships masts can be seen piercing the city sky.

The history of the river, so rich and so inextricably bound up with the growth of the town, is additionally illustrated through all manner of indoor exhibitions. One of the most fascinating is the 'Emigrants to a New World' exhibition which tells the story of nine million emigrants who left their homes in Europe to undertake the hazardous crossing to America

Details in brick and iron, Merseyside Maritime Museum

between 1830 and 1890. Here you can trace their experiences in Liverpool and relive them a little on a reconstruction of a Liverpool quay and a full-size 'tween deck of 'Shackamaxon' an American sailing ship out of Philadelphia in 1854.

Visitors can also tour the Piermaster's House, its interior recreated through the memories of men and women who had lived there as children and see the Cooperage and watch the making of the barrels in which cargoes used to be packed.

Outside, there are more reminders of the days of the tall ships in the cranes and cargo barrels lined up on the granite sets of the quays. They evoke the atmosphere so vividly described by Kohl in 1842: 'These marine parades are genuine Liverpool promenades. Their trees are masts; their flower beds and parterres are groups of tar barrels, tea chests and tobacco casks; the occasional vistas that open carry the eye along the rows of warehouses ...'

(Top photographs) Interiors of the Piermaster's House
(Above) Quayside exhibit, Merseyside Maritime Museum

Monumental river walling alongside Albert Dock

The docks are grand places for contrasting and complementary textures, for the play of light and shade. As well as those afforded by the water, brick and stone, look out for cast iron too - the black bars and pillars of the swing bridges (one with a roadway of wooden sets cut from the heartwood), the capstans and cranes, chains, balusters and lamp standards and, everywhere, bollards exhibiting an unbelievable variety of satisfying shapes, each with a special function but standing today like a sculpture in a maritime park.

We owe quite a debt to Jesse Hartley. Said the Times obituarist of 1860: 'as a dock engineer ... he is admitted to have occupied a high, if not indeed the highest position of any man who has lived within the present century . . . in the design and construction of the numerous docks of Liverpool he has left monuments of his skills as an engineer which will endure at least as long as the fame and commercial prosperity of the port.

PALACES OF COMMERCE

In the early years of the port's commercial explosion, merchants conducted their businesses from homes near the river or from living quarters in their close-packed warehouses. The concept of an office block was unknown in the eighteenth century. However, as prosperity increased, so did the status of those who helped create it - and the status of the buildings that housed their enterprises. Gradually, businessmen moved their domestic residences out to new mansions in the hills above Liverpool whilst, in the city centre, they established their counting houses in fine new buildings - symbols of their financial power - for the first time architect designed and befitting what Picton described as 'the dignity of commerce'.

These latter-day merchant princes had long compared themselves to the self-made men of the Italian Renaissance, to such glittering figures

Cockerell's Bank of England (now a branch of the Trustees Saving Bank)

as the Medicis of Florence or the Doges of Venice. Already, in 1786, they were calling the area before the Town Hall 'the Rialto, where merchants most do congregate', in clear reference to Renaissance Europe's busiest money market. What could be more natural than to imitate such illustrious predecessors in their commercial success, their control of city government, their regard for art and architecture, their admiration of ancient Greece and Rome? And what more natural when building a house of business than to raise it in the style of a Renaissance palace?

In Brunswick Street, which runs up from The Strand, two early examples face each other on opposite corners of Fenwick Street. Halifax House, as it is now called, was built for the Liverpool Union Bank, whose coat of arms is carved on the Fenwick Street facade and bears the date 1835. Executed in the style of palazzo, note the classical upper windows and the monumental cornice.

Opposite, in pale stone is the plain and solid Barclay's Bank. Its ground floor is rusticated, that is to say the courses between the blocks of stone are recessed to produce shadows and an impression of greater strength at the base - very important in a bank! As indicated by the one word carved in stone capitals over the door, 'BANK', this distinguished building retains its original use. It was built as a private bank for Arthur Heywood and Sons, in 1800, and is still known as Heywood's Branch.

If you did not build 'palazzo' at this time you built classical, perhaps a Graeco-Roman temple to house your bank tellers. Dramatically framed at the top of Brunswick Street is the Liverpool branch of the Bank of England (now the Trustees Saving Bank). It was built in 1845 by Charles Robert Cockerell, one of the foremost classical architects of the day. His design demonstrates an inspired melding of classical grandeur and sound practicality.

The Bank of England stands in Castle Street, Liverpool's premier street of business. The thoroughfare takes its name from the thirteenth century castle which stood at its south end, on what is now Derby Square and the site of the Victoria Monument.

The Nelson Monument in Exchange Flags

(Right) The Town Hall, one of the
finest Georgian public buildings
in England
(Below Right) Water Street, one
of the original medieval streets

Castle Street is one of the seven original streets of the town which were laid out at the beginning of the thirteenth century, shortly after King John decided to make Liverpool his port of embarkation for the conquest of Ireland and began 'developing' the small fishing hamlet. The other ancient streets are Dale Street, Water Street. Chapel Street, Tithebarn Street, Old Hall Street and High Street (the last nowadays no more than a parking bay beside the Town Hall).

England's Civil War began the destruction of the medieval castle and the 'improvers' of the early eighteenth century finished the job, replacing it with a church in 1726. Some fifty years later, an American visitor, Samuel Curwen, found Liverpool's streets, 'long, narrow, crooked and dirty' but in 1785 the Town Council began beautifying the central streets and public buildings. First on the list was Castle Street which was widened to its present generous proportions.

At its northern end, dominating the noble prospect, is Liverpool's fine Georgian Town Hall. Designed by John Wood of Bath and built 1749-54, it was seriously damaged by fire in 1795. James Wyatt rebuilt it, adding the dome on which sits a gilded figure of Minerva, goddess of wisdom, her throne supported by dolphins and sea shells - favourite decorative motifs hereabouts. Later, with the elder John Foster, Wyatt added the two-storey Corinthian portico which gives grandeur to the whole.

The original purpose of the building was to act as an exchange on the ground floor where merchants could transact their business while the Town Council had the use of the rooms above. Consequently, Exchange Flags is the name of the square to the rear of the Town Hall. In its centre is the Nelson Monument, Liverpool's first public sculpture, erected in 1813. The drum on which it stands was designed as a ventilation shaft for an underground bonded warehouse: it now performs the same function for an underground car park. Viewed from this side, the Town Hall is

especially elegant with upper loggia surmounted by four classical figures which came from the Irish Houses of Parliament in Dublin.

Classical and Renaissance Classical were Liverpool's favoured styles and many fine examples remain such as

The Albany (1856) in Old Hall Street, Hargreaves Building in Tithebarn Street and Queen Insurance in Dale Street. But as the century progressed, other tastes manifested themselves. The Cooperative bank in Castle Street is an excellent example of the Loire style. Built in 1892 as the Adelphi

*The Albany Building,
'that noble pile of buildings'*

29

Bank and designed by WD Caroe, its contrasting bands of pink sandstone and pale granite combine with mullioned lights and statuary in niches to create a lively, romantic effect. A particularly fine feature are the bronze doors designed by Stirling Lee.

In a similar style is the White Star Building on the corner of The Strand and James Street. Tall and narrow, its alternating bands of pink brick and white stone, its tourelles and cupolas and delicate baroque balconies give these offices the look of a French chateau. The building was designed by the influential architect, Norman Shaw, whose earlier work included New Scotland Yard, on which the White Star was based.

Dale Street with its contrasting architectural styles

During the war, the main gable (to The Strand) was damaged and rebuilt to a simple style, but should you wish to see its former glory, you need only go as far as Dale Street, where J Francis Doyle, a disciple of Shaw, incorporated the design in his giant office block for the Royal Insurance Company, built 1897 - 1903. This impressive building conceals a steel frame of advanced design beneath a traditional exterior in granite and Portland stone. Its crowning feature - and city landmark - is a campanile with sundial, octagonal cupola and gilded dome.

Next but one along Dale Street stands a typical example of late Gothic by the arch-exponent of the style, Alfred Waterhouse. The Prudential Assurance Building was erected in 1885-6 (the tower was added in 1906) in striking red brick and terracotta.

While prominent architects working in accepted styles are well represented in Liverpool, the city is also notable for its remarkable willingness to

innovate, to encourage talented designers brave enough to try the unorthodox. Back on The Strand, at the corner of Water Street stands one of the country's first steel-framed buildings, Tower Building by W Aubrey Thomas. Finished in 1908, it predates his other work, the Royal Liver, and shows a strong functional emphasis with its large windows and exterior cladding of 'self-cleaning' white glazed tiles. It lives up to its name - three towers face the river - but, in fact, it derives from the medieval Tower of Liverpool, belonging to the Stanley family, Earls of Derby, which stood on this site until it was demolished in 1819.

A little higher up the hill, at 14 Water Street, stands what Pevsner calls 'one of the most remarkable buildings of its date in Europe.' Oriel Chambers was built in 1864, yet its facades are almost entirely of glass, a striking prophecy of office blocks to come.

Viewed today, it seems immensely elegant. Tall oriel windows in graceful frames of gilded cast iron terminate in golden finials and fleurs de lys. They are separated by slender stone mullions, decorated with an Early English nail-head design, which rise from first floor level straight to the pinnacled parapet.

Viewed in the 1860s, it appeared quite differently, 'that large agglomeration of plate glass bubbles, this vast abortion', ranted The Builder's critic of 1866.
Oriel Chambers has since become a much celebrated building - little comfort to its long-dead architect, Peter Ellis, who seems to have begun calling himself 'civil engineer' rather than architect, after widespread contemporary condemnation. His building's significance lies in both its technical and stylistic originality. As Quentin Hughes points out in his book 'Seaport', Oriel Chambers is one of the earliest attempts to break away from the classical tradition of commercial architecture. Nor is it really Gothic Revival, except in so far as it embodies the Gothic principal of large expanses of glass and slim stone

mullions. Ellis was able to have so much plate glass because he constructed his building on a cast iron framework (compare the Crystal Palace) and realised that he did not need massive external walls as well. He believed in functionalism and demonstrated that belief honestly and logically. As a result, the office workers in Oriel Chambers enjoyed a great deal of natural light (the absence of which in some of Liverpool's palazzos must have been sorely trying) while Ellis was roundly castigated. Before that happened, however, he had probably finished 16 Cook Street, another remarkable structure, displaying plenty of plate glass (the front looks like a giant Venetian window). Both here and at Oriel Chambers, the rear elevations, clad and cantilevered as they are, show, even more clearly, Ellis's prophetic quality. The design of 16 Cook Street also incorporated a remarkably modern-looking glass-enclosed spiral staircase at the rear. Had Ellis's innovative ideas been better received, an original (rather than revivalist) style of Victorian architecture might have emerged in Britain.

Ellis's Cook Street building, his last documented commission

India Buildings, a powerful expression in neo-classical style by Herbert Rowse

Liverpool's willingness to experiment did not stifle the city's deep attachment to the classical tradition which boldly re-asserted itself in the early twentieth century. On the opposite side of Water Street, in gleaming white Portland Stone, is India Buildings, designed by Herbert J Rowse, leading exponent of the Classical Revival. This office block, one of Liverpool's largest, was built for Holt's Blue Funnel Line at a cost of £1.25 million between 1923 and 1931. From the outside, it looks like a gigantic Roman Villa (from the river you can see its shallow-pitched, green pantiled roofs). Inside is a barrel-vaulted arcade, glowing with colour. The coffered ceiling is in apple green, gold and white; floor and walls are of cream marble and, set in the walls, like a series of picture frames, are bronze shop fronts, beautifully ornamented with rosettes, pine cones, acanthus and oak leaves. Especially evocative of the twenties are the discreetly lit bronze signs that project from each shop.

The barrel-vaulted arcade running through the centre of India Buildings

On the other side of the street, Rowse has given us yet another magnificent building, similarly monumental in scale and with an even more sumptuous interior. Martin's Bank Building, constructed between 1927 and 1932, is French Classical under American influence - Rowse had travelled extensively in North America and his India Buildings also show a strong kinship with transatlantic office design of the period. The exterior is faced in Portland stone and decorated with highly stylised sculptures of sea-gods and dolphins. In, through lovely period revolving doors, past upturned. Art Deco standard-lamps, and

Details, Martin's Bank Building, Water Street

36

suddenly you are in a Roman atrium, a lofty marble hall, surrounded with beautiful colonnades, through which other halls can be seen. The floor is of inlaid marble, with richly coloured geometric borders in green, honeycomb yellow, pink and brown. In the centre stands the circular public counter, a grand affair in purple, vert antico and black marble with ornamental grills of gold bronze. Light floods down from a glazed opening in the centre of the ceiling; around it glows vivid plasterwork in gold, turquoise and red.

No detail has been overlooked; examine the customer writing desks, their supports in gold bronze designed after the ancient Egyptian style. Note their tops, inlaid with chequered patterns, the marquetry racks for bank forms and the gilded desk lights. This building is now the local head office for Barclays Bank and is open to the public during banking hours.

As the nineteenth century progressed, prestigious commercial buildings multiplied in this boomtown of the British Empire. A few are mentioned here but there are many more to see. unique monuments to an age of unprecedented invention and expansion in a once obscure fishing village that became seaport to the world.

The wide range of building styles throughout the commercial sector is a continual source of interest. Here, in Whitechapel, a French influence prevails

The Midland Railway Goods Office

The Mersey Tunnel entrance, a marvel of inter-war engineering

The facade of Exchange Station, now fronting the successful Mercury Court development

The commercial centre from St Johns Gardens

The south facade of St George's Hall, the greatest classical monument of the nineteenth century

TEMPLES OF CULTURE

If you arrive in Liverpool by inter-city train, your first sight of the city is a dramatic one: a great, free-standing Grecian temple confronts you at the main exit from Lime Street Station. Beside it lies a forum while, flanking it to the north, stands a series of splendid neo-classical buildings. All are civic structures; all are dedicated to culture, the arts and education. Together they constitute a brilliant heritage yet, just a generation before the first was built, the contemplation of such an enterprise, let alone its execution, seemed the most remote of possibilities.

By the end of the eighteenth century, Liverpool was a place famed for its riches - and notorious for its philistinism. Devoted as they were to moneymaking, the men of substance in this rough trading town showed little interest in culture or municipal benefaction.

A society for the encouragement of the Arts of Painting and Design was started in 1773 but soon died through lack of interest. In 1810, £1,000 was offered for the erection of a permanent Academy of Art, but nothing came of it.

Details of the Corinthian columns

The citizenry preferred barbarous amusements: bull-baiting, cock fighting and pugilistic encounters. 'What could we expect', wrote James Stonehouse, a former slaveship

41

master, 'when we opened no book to the young and employed no means of imparting knowledge to the old, deriving our prosperity from two great sources, the slave trade and privateering? Swarming with sailormen, flushed with prize-money, was it not likely that the inhabitants generally would take a tone from what they beheld and quietly countenanced?'

Then, suddenly, there emerged a group of remarkably civic-minded people whose efforts to civilize the town brought about a conspicuous change. Outstanding among them was Williams Roscoe, son of an innkeeper in Mount Pleasant, a self-taught scholar, author, abolitionist and political activist. With his friends, he founded the Athenaeum, library for scholars, the Botanic Gardens, Liverpool's first institution for the encouragement of scientific studies and, in 1817, the Royal Institution, Colquitt Street, a focus for the study of literature, science and the arts.

Roscoe also wrote a life of Lorenzo de Medici the most famous of the Renaissance princes - known as 'the Magnificent' - and, like himself, a banker, poet and patron of art. In this work, Roscoe put before his contemporaries the picture of another great commercial city of its day - Florence - where civic munificence bestowed upon the arts had brought undying renown. The book made him an international celebrity and, as he had intended, shaped new attitudes in his native town.

By the 1830s, the climate of opinion had so changed that Liverpool Corporation was eager to raise a temple to culture, a magnificent concert hall in which to accommodate the town's Triennial Music Festival, a very grand and highly successful affair, then held in a local church. A competition was launched, in 1839, and 75 architects entered. The winner was Harvey Lonsdale Elmes, a Hampshire man, scarcely 25 years old, an unknown making his first serious attempt in architectural design. The following year, Elmes won a second competition, this time for assize courts on an adjoining site. Under the circumstances, it was decided to combine both functions in one building and Elmes won the right to revise his plans accordingly. Few cities would have had confidence to commission such a professional novice - and such a youthful one at that - to construct so important a public building on so prominent a site, no matter how brilliant the design. Liverpool did. And the design was one of genius. The result of the city's faith and Elmes's endeavours was to produce the country's finest expression of neo-classical architecture and one of the great buildings of the world.

Elmes's mastery of Greek detail produced, in the words of Queen Victoria, a building 'worthy of ancient Athens'

St George's Hall is a remarkable re-creation of the architectural splendour that once graced Athens and Rome: not a slavish, lifeless reproduction but an inspired reworking of the ancient conventions to produce a building of great power and originality. As you leave Lime Street Station, it stands before you: 490 feet in length, monumental and majestic in mellow Darleydale stone.

The south portico is a Greek Temple front, elevated in the ancient manner, high above the level of the street. It is noble and imposing but it is not the main entrance. Unexpectedly, this is on the long side facing Lime Street and is marked by a great portico of 16 gigantic Corinthian columns, crowned not by pediment or dome but a simple windowless attic.

The north end terminates in an elegant apse, while the heavily fenestrated west side of the hall exhibits dignity with a minimum of architectural display. One reason for this restraint is that the western facade is the back of the building. Although

The north end terminates in an apse of attached columns

Following Elmes's premature death, the Concert Hall was completed by CR Cockerell and is considered by many to be the best room in the building

today it enjoys a spacious setting in St John's Garden, it once stood very close to an undistinguished church of the same name which occupied the site until 1897. This was demolished, leaving us an uninterrupted view of a far better building.

The monumental grandeur of St George's Hall is not confined to the exterior. Inside, it is equally splendid.

Beyond the huge bronze doors of the main entrance lies the Great Hall inspired, in all probability, by Blouet's reconstruction of the Baths of Caracalla in Rome, published in 1828. A mighty barrel vault, richly coffered, spans the whole. Below, Corinthian columns of polished red granite range on either side; arches spring between them, connected by a gallery with balustrades of marble and alabaster.

Statues line the walls. A partially sunken floor, intricately patterned in multi-coloured Minton tiles, completes the effect.

Contemporary technology played an important part in the evocation of such ancient splendour. The engineer, Sir Robert Rawlinson, introduced hollow blocks for the vault which reduced the load by several hundred tons. The heating expert, Dr Boswell Reid, devised a most advanced heating and air conditioning system. A more obvious anachronism is the fine organ at the north end of the Great Hall. It had no part in Elmes's vision. He wrote to a friend: 'I hope when you contemplate the finished structure there will be no organ at the end of the hall'. His plan was for a grand vista, from one end of the building to the other - assize court to assize court, from one Judge's Throne to the other down the vast columned length of the hall. It was not to be; the organ was introduced and blocked the view and Elmes did not live to see the completion of his masterpiece. Overworked and consumptive, he died in Jamaica in 1847, aged 33.

In anticipation of his death, Elmes prepared many detailed drawings for his successor to follow. The choice fell on that eminent neo-classicist, CR Cockerell. It is he who was responsible for the most delightful interior in the building, that of the small Concert Hall, contained in the apse at the north end. In this domed, circular room, everything is light and

delicate. Graceful caryatids carry a balcony of exquisite cast-iron basket work that curves in and out between them. There are lacy friezes of papier-maché, mirrors and chandeliers that lend a magical quality to the room. The warm effect of wood-panelled walls, the modest size and decoration all combine to produce an atmosphere of intimacy as welcome as it is unexpected in so stately a building.

In sombre contrast are the two courtrooms. With their deep wells, claustrophobic box-pew construction, fearsome docks and hierarchical terraces for the accommodation of the various players, they convey all too powerfully the awful majesty of Victorian law. They were the scene of countless famous cases - such as the Maybrick murder - from 1852 until their closure over one hundred and thirty years later, when the new Queen Elizabeth Law Courts were opened in Derby Square. The exterior of the building has also experienced a loss and particularly sorry one. The south portico originally displayed a grand sculptural tympanum.

The caryatid gallery and dome of the Concert Hall

Its subject matter, typical of the age and the city, showed, classically personified, 'Commerce and the Arts bearing tribute to Britannia, and Mercury leading Asia, Europe and America, the sword of power in her right hand, while with her left she raises Africa...' Cockerell made the initial sketches which were reworked by England's finest nineteenth century sculptor, Alfred Stevens. Some twenty years ago, the sculpture was removed for safety reasons. It should be restored. The otherwise magnificent south portico is naked without it.

(Above) The west facade of St George's Hall
(Left) The Wellington Column is an exact replica
of the Melville Monument in Edinburgh

St George's Hall is especially fortunate in occupying a site of sufficient size, space and prominence to show it off to advantage. Before it lies St George's Plateau, a wide promenade adorned with recumbent lions, elegant lamp standards supported by entwined dolphins and two equestrian statues of Prince Albert and Queen Victoria (who thought the Hall 'worthy of ancient Athens').

(Above) St George's Plateau. Perhaps the finest civic panorama in Britain (Right) William Brown Street viewed from St Johns Gardens

To the rear is St John's Garden and, to either side, wide carriageways which descend the gentle slope on whose eminence the Hall stands.

Its situation allows one to view each of the four quite differently designed facades of St George's Hall equally well and to appreciate the superb artistic unity of the whole. In 1873, seventeen years after it was finished, Picton declared it '. . . a building which for magnitude, harmony of proportion, beauty of form and elegance of finish may take its place among the noblest architectural works of any age or country'. Nearly one hundred years later, Sir Nikolaus Pevsner agreed, calling it 'the freest neo-Grecian building in England and one of the finest in the world.' The Corporation of Liverpool placed a Latin inscription over the south portico saying that it had here dedicated a place for arts, laws and councils.

When it saw the superlative quality of its first civic endeavour in this field, it was moved to do more. In the years that followed, a group of remarkably good civic buildings, in the classical style, were built to the north of St George's Hall where they form an excellent backdrop for their great companion.

At the top of the hill is the Sessions House (1882-84), designed in a free classical style by F and G Holme. Next comes the Walker Art Gallery, Grecian in style, designed by HH Vale and paid for by the brewer, Andrew Walker, after he became Mayor in 1873. It was opened in 1877 and holds a particularly large and wide collection of paintings, including William Roscoe's Italian Renaissance collection and a number of important Pre-Raphaelite works.

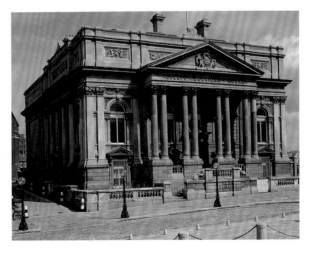

The Sessions House, now the Museum of Labour History

The new Sculpture Room in the Walker Art Gallery

These two buildings stand in Islington; the rest of the row in William Brown Street. The eye finds it difficult to detect any reason for the change of road names but, actually, the two streets run at an angle to one another - a fact cleverly disguised by the design of the next building. This is the Picton Reading Room, a magnificent domed rotunda, edged with a colonnade of Corinthian columns. It was designed by Cornelius Sherlock, opened in 1879 and named after the architect and author, Sir James Picton, then chairman of the Libraries and Museums Committee (and chairman of the first library committee in the country). The interior of the Picton is well worth seeing - splendid galleries, a circular Victorian library with spiralling iron staircases, embarrassing acoustics and other features reminiscent of the Reading Room of the British Museum.

The William Brown Library and Museum was the first to follow St George's Hall and gave the street its present name. It was begun in 1857

The Grecian facade of the Walker Art Gallery with statues of Raphael and Michaelangelo positioned on each side of the entrance

to a design by Thomas Allom and completed, with modifications, by the Corporation Architect, John Weightman, in 1860. Its Corinthian portico is modelled on the south front of St George's Hall and, similarly, a great flight of steps lead up to the entrance. The building was named after its donor, Sir William Brown, a wealthy American cotton merchant in Liverpool. It stands next to the last building to be constructed in the row known as the College of Technology and Museum Extension.

William Brown Library and Museum, originally constructed to hold the Earl of Derby's Natural History Collection

Together, on their spacious and commanding site, these buildings, linked to St George's Hall by a classical fountain and triumphal column, echo the grandeur of an ancient forum. Their presence is perhaps all the more remarkable when one considers that, as late as the end of the eighteenth century, windmills, limekilns and cornfields stood in their place.

The Midland Hotel, Ranelagh Street

54

GIN PALACES

Breweries expanded rapidly in the Victorian era thanks to the Duke of Wellington's Beer House Act of 1830. The purpose of his legislation had been to encourage drinkers to switch from spirits to beer. Instead the sales of both soared - spirits by more than 30%.

In Liverpool, public houses appeared not only on every street corner (as legend has it) but also on every suitable site in between. Most were modest enough to begin with but, by the turn of the century, brewers, like other businessmen, had elevated their establishments into veritable palaces. The city still displays some splendid examples.

The Crown Hotel, on the corner of Lime Street and Skelhorne Street, has an Art Nouveau exterior designed to draw the customers. Plasterwork predominates. Gold lettering announces the hostelry's name on each facade but one: here, in flamboyant manner, a permanent painted plaster advert announces 'Walkers Ales'. The architect of this fine 1905 gin palace is unknown.

The Crown Hotel, Lime Street, with its fine 'Art Nouveau' exterior

(Left) The Vines, Lime Street. An exuberant Edwardian
building with a typically extravagent interior
(Above) Interior detail, The Vines

A little further along Lime Street stands The Vines, an example of Edwardian Baroque in the grand manner. The stone exterior is ornate and interesting but the interior is the place to see. There awaits a magnificent world of mahogany, marble, cut glass and plaster putti, beaten copper and sumptuous carving. The ground floor is set out as a series of rooms - all of different size and character. Some seem private and intimate, others convivial, but the real surprise is the vast cocktail bar at the back of the building. Panelled in mahogany, hung with chandeliers, decorated with period oil paintings, this room recalls the lounge of some luxurious transatlantic liner (indeed, often the same highly skilled Liverpool craftsmen would be responsible for both). The bar's crowning glory is its ceiling, a glass dome surrounded by rich plasterwork, fit to grace the grandest of Edwardian drawing rooms. It is easy to see why The Vines is known locally as 'the big house'. Walter Thomas was the architect of this exuberant extravaganza of 1907.

Thomas's best work as brewery architect was completed a few years before, just a short distance away in Hope Street. This is the Philharmonic Hotel, an Art Nouveau tour de force of turrets, balconies and gilded gates built between 1898 and 1900.

Whereas The Vines' decoration has an angularity, a solid masculine quality about it, The Philharmonic's is sinuous, delicate, ethereal. Splendid gates grace the exterior. These were executed by the English architect, Henry Blomfield Barr, one of a whole team of artists (many from the Liverpool School of Art) who created the superb decorations to be found in this public house.

Gate detail, The Philharmonic Hotel

The magnificent Philharmonic Hotel gates, crafted by H Blomfield Barr

Interior, Philharmonic Hotel

As you step inside, the dramatic sweep of a circular bar arrests your gaze. It is decorated with floral mosaics and must be one of the few bars to retain its brass footrail. From the tessellated floor to the ornamented ceiling, architectural decoration in flowing fantastic forms command attention: sculpture, plasterwork, metalwork, woodwork, all in perfect unity, all executed to the highest standards. No corner is neglected, not even the gentlemen's lavatories which are famed for their marble opulence (the women's, however, are thoroughly disappointing).

There are scores of interesting public houses to discover in Liverpool. The Midland Hotel and Central Hotel (both in Ranelagh Street), the Lisbon, in Victoria Street and the Lion Tavern, on the corner of Moorfields, are just a few of the many hostelries worth visiting.

GRACIOUS LIVING

Rodney Street was one of the first of the new residential areas that Liverpool's wealthy merchants created for themselves at the end of the eighteenth century. It was also one of the largest and, to our great good fortune, survives virtually intact today. Building began about 1780. The street's name is a sure indication of the date of its foundation, commemorating as it does the naval victory of Lord Rodney over the Comte de Grasse. Development was slow at first but, by the turn of the century, Liverpool's rich and respectable traders were deserting the hurly burly of the downtown area and flocking to Rodney Street to enjoy a more gracious style of living and what doctors deemed 'better air', on the edge of a then rural environment.

The new residents were not disappointed. While the poor colonised the cellars of their former homes to live in filthy, lightless, lethal

Doorway, Rodney Street

conditions, the merchants built airy apartments within elegant exteriors from end to end of the fine Georgian street. Surely no era has handled domestic architecture more successfully or more satisfyingly from an aesthetic point of view than that which produced Rodney Street. It remains a delightful place to live,

work or walk in, a place where the buildings are human and harmonious in their proportions, where the building materials of brick, wood and stone are pleasingly used in relation to one another and where the decorative detail is of sufficient quantity, variety and quality to arouse and hold our interest. The doorcases are

particularly arresting and worthy of study. There are many subtle variations; some have pediments, other are roundheaded with delicate fanlights; some have porticos with stepped, railed entrances; some are in wood, others in stone; some are supported by Doric columns, others by Ionic, some are fluted, some plain.

The doors of Rodney Street

These are not the only decorative features worth inspecting. Several of the houses have balconies, executed in iron, the fashionable material of the day. Again there is variety of pattern; ornamental chains grace those of number 48, while 50 - 54 have semi-circular balconies with an open basketwork design.

Some splendid lighting fixtures survive in addition to the street lamp standards. Number 34 has two fine standard lampholders on either side of the railings leading to the entrance; between numbers 50 and 52 there is a wall-mounted version. Other cast iron features include boot scrapers, conveniently set into front-door steps for the use of muddy footed callers (of which there must have been a great

many in Rodney Street's early years).

Many of the houses have associations with famous people - and usually display a plaque accordingly. Number 35 is thought to be the first house built in Rodney Street, said to

be on land leased from William Roscoe. It is a large, five-bay house with a pediment over its whole width. The doorway is also pedimented and elegantly carved - note the swags that decorate the frieze. In 1799, Liverpool's Mayor lived here.

On the other side of the street, at number 62, is another fine house of similar size, built as a detached property in 1796. Here was born, in 1808, one of Britain's most famous prime ministers, William Ewart Gladstone. At the other end of the

(Left) Mornington Terrace, Upper Duke Street
(Below) Gambier Terrace, probably designed by
John Foster Junior and built 1832-7

street, at number 9, the poet
Arthur Clough was born in 1819 and,
a year later, his sister Anne, who was
to become the first principal of
Newnham College, Cambridge.

In 1873, Picton reported that
Rodney Street was having a struggle to
maintain its respectability - medical
men had arrived - shopkeepers had
moved in! He feared the worst,
predicting shopfronts and the
inevitable triumph of the trader.
The doctors are still there, now joined
by architects and there are a few
shops at one end but people still live
in Rodney Street, which not only
retains its charm but is now one of
thirty conservation areas in the city.

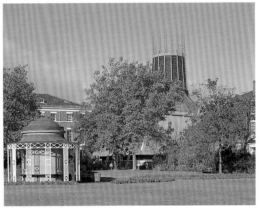

(Left) Falkner Square
*(Above) Abercromby Square with its central garden house
is now an elegant part of the University*

Two cathedrals on opposite ends of Hope Street

CATHEDRAL CITY

Liverpool has not one, but two cathedrals. They stand within sight of one another, at opposite ends of the same street which, by happy chance, bears the name of Hope Street.

Remarkably, both cathedrals were built in the same century and, even more remarkably, that century was our own. There, any similarity ends. Denominationally, one is Anglican, the other Roman Catholic. Stylistically, they could hardly be more different. The Anglican Cathedral, romantic and monumental, rises like some great medieval fortress upon its rocky cliff: the Catholic Cathedral, product of the space age that it is, looks like a gigantic Apollo capsule on the launch-pad, waiting for lift-off into the cosmos.

Despite the very different routes taken by their respective architects, both buildings succeed in communicating a powerful spirituality.

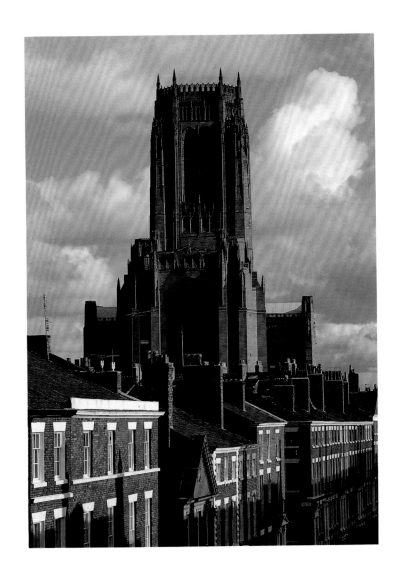

The Anglican Cathedral viewed from the Georgian elegance of Rodney Street

Although entirely twentieth century in its construction, the Cathedral is the last, great monument of the Gothic Revival

The Anglican Cathedral, begun in 1904 and over seventy years in the building, commands a superb site, high above the river on St James's Mount, one of Liverpool's several hills. On the west side, the ground slopes gently down towards the city centre; on the east, it falls away steeply to form a craggy gorge which seems to serve the towering Gothic structure as an immense dry moat.

The effect of this setting is highly picturesque, although its origins are rather more prosaic. The 'gorge' began as a quarry (stone for the Town Hall was excavated here) but, by 1825, it has been exhausted. The architect, John Foster Junior, then stepped in with the inspired notion of turning it into a cemetery. The result was spectacular.

Imagine a wooded, grassy hollow, studded with obelisks, urns, railed vaults and other funerary monuments, threaded with paths and bordered by catacombs hewn in the sides of its sheer walls. Tombs tunnelled in the eastern face were reached by great terraced ramps, wide enough to take the grandest of funeral processions, complete with hearse and plumed horses.

The ramps may still be walked today, together with the rest of the rocky depths but, sadly, most of the 'chaste and elegant monuments erected to departed worth' were swept away in the 1970's so that a sanitised park could take the place of this dramatic nineteenth century necropolis.

Nevertheless, Liverpool society of that bygone age is still vividly reflected in the remaining memorial stones. Sea captains abound - several American, like Captain Elisha Lindsay Halsey of Carorlina (sic) whose misspelt monument of 1844 bears the star spangled banner. The Keay family were most unfortunate: David died, aged 19, on his homeward passage from Philadelphia in 1834; his brother, Captain James Keay, died three years later 'at Africa', aged 28; another two years and the family lost Thomas, aged 19, 'at Demerara'. Their father, Captain Alexander Keay, outlived them all, dying ten years after, aged 62. 'Blessed are they who die in the Lord', comments the gravestone stoically.

The skills of the local stonemasons are evident throughout the cathedral

The loss of children is much in evidence. Tombstones erected by the Orphan Boys' Asylum and the Liverpool Bluecoat Hospital list infants, children and teenagers - an indication of the poor hygiene, poor nutrition and limited medical knowledge, as well as evidence of poverty amid the riches.

A short distance away in this once fashionable burial ground, stand the monuments of the great: polished granite pilasters for William Brown, Bart., donor of the Museum and Library; a classical rotunda for William Huskisson MP who, having promoted the building of the world's first passenger railway, from Liverpool to Manchester, was tragically - and incredibly - killed by it when Stephenson's Rocket ran him over on opening day in1830. The fine statue of Huskisson that once stood in the mausoleum (and which everyone complained could not be properly seen there) has been removed to the Walker Art Gallery.

In death, as in life, nineteenth-century society preserved the strict distinctions of an hierarchical age.

However, little could be done about the overcrowding in the cemetery and, until the recent landscaping, it was plain that all were packed together, cheek by jowl. Above, in the cathedral, the living were to enjoy space in abundance. Over 600 feet in length, with a tower soaring 331 feet above floor level, the Liverpool Cathedral Church of Christ is truly immense. It is said to be largest Anglican church in the world and, certainly, it is the sheer scale of the building which makes an immediate impact and remains in the memory.

New cathedrals are rare events (Liverpool's was the first to be consecrated in England on a wholly new site since the thirteenth century) and not even the ever-confident Victorians expected to see one, let alone anything to rival the work of medieval masters. However, the idea took shape when Liverpool finally achieved city-status in 1880 and became a diocese in its own right (prior to this time it was under the jurisdiction of the Bishop of Chester). In 1885, Parliament authorised the building of a cathedral.

The High Altar, Anglican Cathedral

The site originally chosen was St John's Gardens, behind St George's Hall. Fortunately, these plans came to nothing. Eventually, the present site was secured and an architectural competition launched in 1902. Although the Building Committee dropped their controversial demands that all designs should be Gothic (by then an outmoded style), architects who wanted to win knew what was required of them.

In the event, a 22 year-old triumphed, the virtually unknown Giles Gilbert Scott, who was later knighted for his efforts. Once again, the city had chosen a talented youth to build one of its grandest monuments - just as it had chosen Elmes for St George's Hall some 60 years before. Scott started work in 1904 on this great swan-song of the Gothic Revival and was still busy on the unfinished structure when he died in 1960, in his eightieth year. It was not until 1978, that a service to mark the completion of the gargantuan task could finally be held.

The main entrance, or West Door as it is traditionally called in cathedral architecture, was the last part to be built. Work began at the opposite end and slowly, painstakingly, made its way forward, with Scott radically revising his original design in the process. The building material, red sandstone, was mainly quarried in the city, at Woolton, and the craftsmen who worked it with such consummate skill were mostly Liverpool men.

When you enter, you realise that the interior of this cathedral is unlike that of any other in the Gothic style. Most strikingly, there are no pillars to interrupt the view from West Door to East Window. This allows the vast length and height to combine to produce a spatial grandeur, at once dramatic and awe-inspiring. Another unusual feature is the bridge that spans the nave. It is a romantic touch and one of great strength, more reminiscent of a castle than a church: note the jettied balcony of carved oak, not unlike a minstrel's gallery.

Through the arch, glowing in the light from the West Window, can be seen the gilded panels of the magnificent high altar screen. To the right of this, through a small door in the South Aisle, is the Lady Chapel. This was the first part of the cathedral to be built and has quite a different feel from the rest. Although it is much more ornate, the decoration is delicate and pretty, clearly displaying the influence of William Morris and the Arts and Crafts Movement. Especially pleasing is the carved and painted wooden altar screen or reredos with its Gothic shepherds and angels, filagree frame, canopies and twining golden lilies of the Virgin.

High up, at the other end of the chapel is a delightfully carved organ loft and organ with trumpet-blowing angels on either side. The heads of musician angels look down from the chapel walls and, beneath, an elaborately carved text from the Gospel of St John beginning: 'God so loved the world that he gave his only begotten Son...' Golden Gothic lanterns light the whole and an excellent view of these and the whole area can be had from the chapel gallery.

The Dulverton Bridge spanning the nave adds a romantic touch to the vast interior

The cathedral's oldest piece of sculpture, a kneeling life-size madonna by Renaissance artist, Luca della Robbia, adorns the altar steps of the Lady Chapel. The rest is contemporary with the building, much of it by E Carter Preston, including the baptismal font with its beautifully chosen water-effect marble.

As you leave the cathedral by the West Porch, note John Foster's fine Mortuary Chapel, or Oratory, of 1829. Built in Liverpool's favourite style of the period - the classical - Foster's chapel is a perfect Greek temple in replica.

(Left) The High Altar and Reredos
(Below) The Musicians Window

73

Less than half a mile away, the Roman Catholic Cathedral offers a completely contrasting experience. Modern in design and materials, it is built not on traditional cruciform lines but in the round. A gigantic central cylinder is capped by a conical aluminium-clad roof and, resting on it, is a multi-coloured, cylindrical, glass lantern, weighing nearly 1,000 tons, which supports a delicate crown of cross-tipped pinnacles. White, tessellated flying buttresses join reinforced concrete roof trusses in a dramatic upward thrust. Between them, stand side-chapels, baptistry and porches - in all, sixteen differentiated structures - which surround the central area to form the external walls of the cathedral.

The main approach is via a great right-angled ramp and staircase, like the ascent to some ancient Aztec holy place. At the top, the illusion is reinforced by a powerfully carved, monolithic bell-tower and, set in it, a main door embellished with images of primitive force. Look more carefully, however, and, on the tower, can be discerned the Christian symbolism of the three crosses; on the door, the emblems of the four evangelists.

Inside, the entrance hall seems remarkably plain and undistinguished but dramatic effects are never far away in this memorable building. The hall proves to be simply a prelude to the most spectacular of them. Beyond its doors, the lofty arena of the cathedral proper is suffused in blue light: in the centre, a pure white marble altar confronts the gaze: above it, suspended in the air, a great crown of thorns reminds the faithful of their Saviour's Passion.

(Above) The Metropolitan Cathedral of Christ the King

(Left) Interior, Metropolitan Cathedral
(Below) Details of the organ

In terms of decoration, the interior is comparatively bare, yet the religious symbolism is strong - perhaps all the stronger for it. There are medieval echoes in the brightly coloured banners and fabric pictures that adorn the plain concrete walls. Above all, it is the stained glass that is responsible for producing so many of the impressive effects found here. It frames each separate chapel with bands of brilliant azure: with the chapels, different colours create different moods - a bright blaze of red by the confessionals, warm white light in the Lady Chapel, while yellow and blue dapple the walls of the Chapel of the Blessed Sacrament.

Multi-coloured light floods down from the lantern, designed by John Piper and executed by Patrick Reyntiens. As the seasons pass, as each day progresses, the colours change, imparting to the cathedral different moods, evocative powers, a living quality of its own.

The Metropolitan Cathedral of Christ the King - to give this church its full title - took just five years to complete. It is the work of Sir Frederick Gibberd who, in 1960, won the competition to find a suitable design. The conditions stipulated that the congregation of over 2,000 should have a full view of the celebrant and that the building costs should be no more than £1 million with a completion time within ten years.

Consecrated in 1967, the cathedral has become a significant feature on the Liverpool skyline. Although in marked contrast to its Anglican neighbour, the two together dominate the landscape for miles around, in a spirit of ecumenicism for which the city has become so famous in recent years.

In its nineteenth century heyday, Liverpool had no cathedral of either denomination but it abounded in other places of worship - well over fifty churches and chapels in the city centre alone, in 1836. Every style of architecture was represented from pure gothic, to elegant confections in the manner of Sir Christopher Wren, to pure classicism. Many have gone, swept away by development, redundancy and the Second World War, which destroyed so much of the city. Others, fortunately, remain.

A miraculous survivor is the church of Our Lady and St Nicholas. Known irreverently, but affectionately, as St Nick's, this is the Liverpool Parish Church and it stands at the bottom of Chapel Street, close by the Pier Head, looking out across the river. St Nicholas is the patron saint of sailors and it is said that they would come here to present an offering for a prosperous voyage and a safe return.

Of the oldest foundation by far of any church in city, it was built in the middle of the fourteenth century as a

Our Lady and St Nicholas.

chapel-of-ease under Walton until 1699, when Liverpool was made a distinct parish. However, the oldest part of the existing church is the steeple, built by Thomas Harrison of Chester, 1811-15. This is a delightful essay in early Gothic Revival; a delicate little spire, surmounted by a

ship weather vane rises from an octagonal open lantern. Flying buttresses connect this to a pinnacle at the four corners of the tower.

It was built to replace the original spire which fell down 'with a terrible crash' on the 11th February 1810,

St Michael-in-the Hamlet, an exercise in cast-iron construction

killing 22 girls from a charity school, who were walking up the aisle for morning service. The rest of the church was destroyed in World War II. The rebuilding dates from 1952.

Dating from the same period but of an essentially different and wholly remarkable character is the church of St Michael-in-the-Hamlet, Aigburth. It was built in 1814 and everything that could be was executed in iron. Window tracery, door and window surrounds, cladding of the clerestory, external buttress copings, parapets, finials - all are of iron.

St Michael's was the result of a collaboration between two friends. One was the architect Thomas Rickman - a pharmacist turned surgeon turned clerk, born in Berkshire, but who had to leave the south of England through debt and, in 1807, came to Liverpool to look for work. He became an accountant, pursued a host of hobbies - including architecture - and in 1812 was elected Professor of Architecture, at the Liverpool Academy. The other friend was John Cragg, proprietor of the Mersey Iron Foundry and a man with an obsessional interest in the architectural application of cast iron. A partnership was born.

Their first excursion into cast iron church construction was St George's, in Everton. All the requisite parts were prefabricated in Cragg's foundry - columns, window tracery, vaulting ribs - and bolted together on site. The style was Gothic and Rickman, through his subsequent writings, was to become a major influence on the Gothic revival of the nineteenth century.

St Michael's was their second church. It contained even more cast iron than the first, roused a good deal of controversy and became known as the 'cast iron church'. It was joined by a group of five cottages - which also used cast iron wherever possible - which Cragg built in the creation of St Michael's Hamlet, now a conservation area and still picturesque and secluded. The duo went on to build a third church, almost literally out of the

St Agnes, Ullet Road, is a magnificent late Victorian church

same mould, St Philip's in Hardman Street, 1816 (since demolished). Between them they gave rise to the development of the prefabricated cast iron churches that were exported from Liverpool and other British ports for congregations as far afield as America and Australia.

As the century progressed, these early examples of Gothic Revival were joined by scores of others. One of the most impressive late Victorian examples is the church of St Agnes in Ullet Road. Built in 1883, its exterior is of red brick, its interior of stone. The style is thirteenth century Gothic.

John Pearson, architect of Truro Cathedral, was responsible for the design. The church is complemented by a Hall and Vicarage, built four years later by Norman Shaw.

Also in Ullet Road, stands the Unitarian Church of 1896-1902 by Thomas and Percy Worthington, themselves Unitarians from Manchester. Many famous Liverpool families - the Rathbones, Holts, Booths, Roscoes - were associated with the denomination at this time and the building is one of the most ambitious Unitarian churches in the land. Red brick with stone dressings form the building material but it is more noteworthy for its Art Nouveau features, especially the west doors of beaten copper by Richard Rathbone and the light fittings. In addition, there is stained glass by William Morris & Company, a bust of Roscoe by Gibson, dated 1834, and a monument of 1874 to William Rathbone by Foley.

There are many more fine examples of ecclesiastical architecture in Liverpool. Some are no longer

churches but have found new uses, for example, St Bride's in Huskisson Street. Built, in 1830, by Samuel Rowlands in the form of a Greek temple, this is one of the few remaining representatives of its splendid kind which was so hugely popular in Liverpool. A later example of the classical style is the former congregational church in Great George Street, built 1840-41 by Joseph Franklin. This distinguished building, with its semi-circular porch of monumental proportions and giant Corinthian columns, has been completely rebuilt inside to serve as a community arts centre.

Interior, St Agnes

One church, St Luke's at the bottom of Leece Street, is preserved as a ruin. Designed in 1802, by John Foster Senior, it was completed by his son, John Foster Junior, in 1831, and bombed in the Second World War. Its Gothic skeleton remains as a memorial. Fast dwindling into a ruin is another fine church by the same architect, St Andrew's Church of Scotland in Rodney Street. This was opened in 1824 and, again, is one of the few remaining examples of the classical style, elegant and austere, with massive Ionic columns supporting a recessed portico between two flanking towers surmounted by domes. The churchyard retains a curious tomb in the form of a pyramid. This building is too good to lose. It should be saved and restored.

One sturdy, if unexpected survivor, that should be better known is the Toxteth Unitarian Chapel. It stands on the corner of Park Road and Ullet Road and dates from 1618. Formerly Presbyterian, it was largely rebuilt in 1774 and a porch added in 1841. Inside there are three galleries and box pews. The Toxteth Chapel was probably the earliest building of significance in this area - a deer park in the middle ages - and provides a tangible, living link with Liverpool's distant past.

Stonework detail, St Agnes

St Luke's Church, a dramatic memorial to the Liverpool blitz,
is a lovely silhouette against the sky

A BREATH OF THE COUNTRY

'If it be true that the stage of civilization reached by any city is, to a great degree, registered by the number of parks which it provides for its poorer citizens, then indeed does Liverpool stand in high place'.

That was the verdict of Black's guidebook to Liverpool for the year 1900, written at a time when the city's parks and recreation grounds accounted for 800 acres. Since then, the acreage has quadrupled to make Liverpool a decidedly verdant city. This may seem strangely at odds with the popular image of England's industrial north but the facts speak for themselves. Liverpool has preserved, intact, some of the finest examples from that golden age of public park design, the Victorian era. And, despite what must be formidable maintenance programmes, the tradition of good gardening on a grand scale has persisted. New parks continue to be laid out, the

most spectacular and ambitious to date being the site of the International Garden Festival, Britain's first-ever venture of its kind, which was held in Liverpool in 1984 and involved the landscaping of 250 acres of derelict land.

Although Liverpool is a city replete with parks, this is far from apparent in the centre of town: only St John's Gardens and the churchyard green of St Nicholas in Chapel Street exist to relieve the streetscape - and both are small and formal. Why should this be? Picton explains: 'The town extended its borders with unexampled rapidity. Long rows of streets climbed up the hill and covered the heath; men were too busy and occupied to think of recreation; and when at length the community woke up to the necessity of some effort being made, lo! the land was gone - absorbed - built on.' So, what is perhaps the most pernicious side-effect of industrialisation, the destruction of the

countryside, took Liverpool by surprise. So too did the ills that followed in its wake: overcrowding, filth, lack of light and air, malnutrition, disease and early death. The scenario was the same in all the new industrial centres of England but, when epidemics of cholera and typhus were spawned by these iniquitous conditions, fear prompted men to action and reforms were urgently sought.

One remedy was to re-create a breath of the country in the claustrophobic new towns by introducing large areas of parkland. These, the Victorians trusted, would promote healthy minds and healthy bodies whilst providing for 'the gratification of contented labour'. In Liverpool, Princes Park was the first venture of this kind. Lying at the end of a Parisian-style boulevard, fine trees shade walks and drives, parting here and there to reveal unexpected vistas - the waters of a lake, the gentle rise of

(Below) Walled garden, Reynold's Park
(Right) Ornate cottage, Sefton Park
(Below Right) Speculative Victorian private estates such as Grassendale and Cressington Parks combined a rural ideal with proximity to the city centre

a hill, an elegant mansion in the distance. Pathways skirt broad lawns and wind their way between variegated shrubberies and plantations.

The design is one of consummate skill, clearly the work of a master. In fact, it is the work of the master of Victorian landscape design, Joseph Paxton - the gardener's boy who rose to become the architect of the Crystal Palace. Princes Park, in 1842, was his first independent commission. He designed it at the behest of Richard Vaughan Yates, a wealthy Liverpool philanthropist, who had bought the land - about 90 acres - from the Earl of Sefton with the express purpose of creating a park but with residential development in and around it. His intention was to pay for the laying out of the park by selling the houses, which would have their value enhanced by their setting. Although this tactic was not immediately successful for Yates, it proved popular and was used again and again - notably in Paxton's next commission, in 1843, on the other side of the Mersey, Birkenhead Park. In each instance, many of the houses are of considerable architectural interest.

The ideas that Paxton displayed in the design of these parks - the careful disposition of trees, water and artificial hills to create seemingly uncontrived views, the introduction of winding paths, romantic grottoes, pavilions and other picturesque features, established the norm for nineteenth century public park design, not only in Britain but in America and Europe.

Despite its being open to the public, Princes Park was privately owned and remained so until the City Council bought it in 1918 (a real snip at £11,000 when it had cost Yates £70,000 to develop seventy-five years before). Birkenhead Park, on the other hand, was the first publicly promoted park in the country, a precedent that set the pattern of future development. In Liverpool, the Council responded with two modest additions, Wavertree Park, in 1854, and Shiel Park, in 1862. By now, parks were deemed a necessity for the

Lark Lane, an attractive Victorian suburb on the fringe of Sefton Park

people and, what with the flush of commercial prosperity that followed the American Civil War, expense became a question of minor importance. A positive mania for parks took hold of the public mind. Bowing to it, the Council voted to form not one but three, large new ones: Stanley Park to the north, Sefton Park to the south and Newsham Park to the east; a total of almost five hundred green and pleasant acres.

The Palm House, Sefton Park

Of all the parks, Sefton is the most successful in creating the illusion of countryside in the middle of a city. Lush grasslands blend into trees; a stream trickles through a wooded vale, winding its way past islands, through rock pools, into a princely lake. So complete is the effect that, in large tracts of the park's 269 acres, man's role in its creation is scarcely discernible. In other parts, human handiwork is explicit: an elegant avenue leads to the Palm House, a glass palace for exotic plants. The Victorians loved conservatories and displayed a genius for building them. The Palm House is a delight. Three tiered, glass domes stand on an octagonal base of polished red granite, their wood and metal work painted white. Inside, giant palms fan their greenery across spiral stairways and wonderfully sentimental marble statuary. The air is warm and moist. Outside, statues of a different kind, depict Darwen, Columbus and other great pioneers. Also worth looking at are the ornamental iron gates, with splendid Art Nouveau flourishes, which stand at the entrances to the Palm House.

The well-to-do and prosperous middle classes sought out the houses around the public parks: the really wealthy had their own private parkland. Calderstones Park began in the second category but ended in the first when the City Council purchased it in 1902. Its 94 acres are well wooded and contain a charming, walled Old English Garden, a Japanese Garden and an intriguing Systematic Garden, where plants are arranged in beds according to their botanical classification. In the middle of Calderstones Park stands the Georgian Mansion House of 1828, of which the park once formed the estate. The park's name derives from the prehistoric Calder Stones which formed part of a burial mound on the site.

Another beautiful estate and historic house became open to all in 1973 when, following the death of the Earl, the Countess of Sefton donated Croxteth Hall and its 500 acre country park for public use. The house dates from 1575 but was rebuilt, in 1702, with a magnificent west front of a most unusual Queen Anne design. East and south wings were added by the Victorians in a gabled Tudor style, with the Edwardians completing the square in 1902. A Victorian Farmyard survives along with a wide variety of estate buildings, many of them restored to working order, which gives a fascinating insight into the life of the Hall in its heyday.

Still older is Speke Hall, a Grade 1 listed Tudor manor house on the southern outskirts of the city, close to Liverpool Airport. It is a surprising find in a town that sacrificed so many of its early buildings to industrial progress but there it stands. Speke Hall was built between 1490 and 1612 and is one of the finest examples of timber framed buildings in Britain. It is typically picturesque: red sandstone for roof, chimneys and garden walls; magnificent expanses of highly decorated half-timbering; leaded lights, barge boards robustly carved and more concern for pattern than strict symmetry. The interior is no less interesting with a profusion of superb oak panelling, decorative carving, plasterwork and, in the Great Parlour, a particularly good stucco ceiling.

Although Liverpool's rapid growth in the nineteenth century quickly engulfed outlying rural settlements, many suburbs have retained their country village character.

Woolton Village is one such area. The first written record of it dates from the Domesday Book, in 1086, and the history of its development can be traced in its buildings. The Old School, in School Lane, dates from the seventeenth century. Woolton Hall, a Grade 1 listed building of sandstone ashlar, dates from 1704 when it provided a grand home for the Molyneux family. In 1774, Robert Adam remodelled the interior and his staircase, decorative plasterwork ceilings and fire surrounds survive. The Hall's splendid porte cochere was a Victorian addition.

In contrast is Ashton Square, a terrace of eighteenth century cottages, built for the Hall's estate workers. These stand in a cul de sac off School Lane. No. 3 still has its original gothic-style leaded lights.

(Above) Speke Hall, one of the finest timber-framed buildings in Britain
(Top Right) The Black Bull, Gateacre
(Centre Right) Cottage, Woolton Village

(Below and Right) Croxteth Hall and Farm. Once the family home of the Earls of Sefton, now owned by the City of Liverpool

Gateacre Village is smaller than Woolton and in marked contrast: here are tightly grouped buildings of sandstone, red brick and striking black and white half-timbering. The Brown Cow and the Black Bull public houses are both typical examples of fanciful Victorian Tudor, while Clegg's Factory on Gateacre Brow is a good example of a picturesque Victorian manufactory. Built in brick with decorative panels of blue and yellow brick, it has a fish-scale slate roof, surmounted by a central louvred lantern, topped with ornate iron cresting and a pretty weather vane.

New 'villages', created from scratch, but combining the rural charm of the hamlet with a certain exclusivity, security and proximity to the urban centre, became extremely popular in the nineteenth century. Grassendale and Cressington Parks are two such developments in Liverpool. Laid out, off Aigburth Road, in the early to mid nineteenth century as a speculative venture, they remain highly desirable residences in the last decade of the twentieth.

CHANGING CITY

Liverpool is known to millions of people across the globe as Beatle City, home of 'the four lads who shook the world' with their music in the 1960s. Each year, fans from many countries visit Liverpool to follow in the footsteps of the Beatles, to see the places commemorated in their songs and where they spent their formative years. Penny Lane, Strawberry Fields and much else of the Beatles's Liverpool remains largely unaltered but, in other respects, a marked change has come over the city. In the centre, the streets have lost their sombre colour: famous and not so famous buildings that the Beatles must have known as soot-clad and begrimed, are now returned to all their pristine glory - white Portland stone, shining granite, honey-coloured sandstone. Liverpool is a cleaner city.

But that is not all. Many of Liverpool's best nineteenth century

buildings are, and continue to be, refurbished and adapted for modern use. The most outstanding example (and the largest Grade I listed building in the country) is, of course, the Albert Dock with its complex of commercial, leisure and residential development. A few years ago these magnificent waterfront buildings sat empty and decaying: now they stand transformed into a superbly attractive and exciting environment, the centre of a new community.

(Far Left) The gates of Strawberry Fields, an essential visit for thousands of Beatles fans
(Left) Stanley Dock. Jesse Hartley's warehouse is scheduled for renovation in the next phase of dockland regeneration

Throughout the docklands, which stretch for 7·5 miles along the waterfront, fine historical buildings are being renovated and converted. Just south of the Albert Dock and slightly inland, stands Wapping Warehouse, built by Hartley in 1856, and another triumphant melding of form and function. As recently as 1982, it was still in service as a bonded liquor store, now it has a new and highly successful use as a private apartment block.

To the north, comprehensive redevelopment is in train in the area of Stanley Dock. On sites occupied by redundant buildings of no architectural interest or merit, clearance and new developments are taking place. In some instances, dock basins have been filled to form new sites or improved for watersports, while services, quaysides and the general environment are all being upgraded. Where the South Docks end, new greenery begins with the beautifully landscaped gardens that are the legacy of the International Garden Festival. A few years ago, this was an area of inaccessible dereliction; now, new roads lead to new houses and an excellent leisure amenity that has opened up superb views of Liverpool's mighty river.

The majestic Adelphi Hotel has undergone a £5 million interior refurbishment. It was well worth the trouble. Completed in 1912 to a design by Frank Atkinson (the architect of Selfridges in London), the Adelphi is a stately affair that looks the way many people feel a big hotel should. Its lines seem to echo those of the great passenger ships of the day - the Lusitania, the Mauretania. Many of the Adelphi's former clients must have sought out the hotel, so comparable in its luxury and decor to the liners, just before or after a transatlantic crossing.

Facing the Adelphi, over the main entrance to Lewis's Department Store, stands that familiar Liverpool landmark, Sir Jacob Epstein's grand-scale sculpture of a nude male figure symbolising Liverpool's resurgence after the devastation it suffered in the Second World War. It is probably the city's most famous statue - celebrated in song as 'a statue exceedingly bare'. Lewis's stands in Ranelagh Street, at a starting point for what is Liverpool's most constantly changing area - at least at street level - the shopping centre.

Amid the frenetic activity can be found the quiet and changeless. Off Church Street, the heart of the retail trade, lies a quaint cobbled courtyard, around which there stands a perfect example of a building in the Queen Anne style. This is Bluecoat Chambers, built in 1717 as a charity school and known as the Bluecoat Hospital or Bluecoat School. Boys and girls still attended as late as 1906

Today, this architectural jewel is a well-established centre for the arts, providing a fine gallery and shops. Concerts take place here, artists have their studios and people come to meet over a meal or simply to sit in the calm oasis of the paved, enclosed garden to the rear.

In contrast to the venerable Bluecoat are the new self-contained developments such as Cavern Walks, an office and shopping centre and St John's Market and Clayton Square shopping malls.

(Above) The Bluecoat Gallery
(Right) The new Clayton Square shopping development

Clayton Square is a product of the late 1980s and, accordingly, displays a return to traditional building values and materials. Although a very old city square was swept away to make this development possible, the new precinct sensitively echoes Victorian architecture in its general design with colour-banded brickwork and, inside

a glorious light-giving glass roof that Paxton would have been proud of, barrel-arched, domed and given added interest by its skeleton of metal ribs. Clayton Square, with its light and airiness, imparts a sense of uplift immediately you enter it - surely a very welcome quality in any building.

Liverpool has a long tradition of excellence in the arts. The Walker Art Gallery has one of the best collections outside of London and the John Moores Exhibition, held every two years, is widely regarded as the barometer of contemporary art in Britain. The Royal Liverpool Philharmonic Orchestra has an international reputation and regularly attracts leading musicians to the city.

The city's outstanding theatrical tradition lives on at the Everyman theatre, which is housed in an early eighteenth century non-conformist chapel. Liverpool's other major repertory company can be found at the Playhouse Theatre, built in 1865 as the Star Music Hall.

Energy and excellence are equally evident in Liverpool's sporting achievements. Since the 1960s, the city has witnessed, year after year, a near domination of the national football scene. Liverpool Football Club have won virtually every trophy worth winning, usually two or three at a time, and Everton are close behind. Such successes are not just passing moments of glory, they are a continuing tradition that has inspired generation after generation.

Tradition is very much part of another great national institution, the Aintree Grand National. Founded in 1837 and dubbed 'Grand National' ten years later, it is held in March each year. This famous steeplechase - over four and a quarter miles and thirty jumps - is the one event guaranteed to empty the streets as millions watch the annual ritual of riders being unseated whilst tackling a course of frightening severity.

(Top) Liverpool versus Everton. The match that really matters in Britain's football city
(Centre) The Grand National. Now over 150 years old and still the most popular of all horse races
(Bottom) Liverpool Playhouse

(Right) The Victoria Building – the original 'red brick University'
(Below) The Student Union Building, University of Liverpool. An elegant design by Charles Reilly

In the 1980s, Liverpool has begun to display great skill in blending the old with the new to the advantage of both. Mercury Court, the Exchange Station redevelopment is one such example. The Albert Dock and other dock developments, together with new-build projects are in contrasting ways, successful in adding a new sense of purpose to the city. So too, is Wavertree Technology Park, located two miles from the city centre. This 64 acre site is the home of a new community of high-tech enterprises and has been designed specifically to meet their needs. It is an attractive low density development, set in a landscaped park, that offers its occupants an impressive range of centrally managed services.

Increasingly, in such developments, Liverpool University plays a key role. Pioneering research work, plus involvement in its commercial application, is bringing the University increasing success in attracting grant awards and broadening its sphere of influence. At the same time, traditional academic disciplines retain their popularity for students. This mix of the old and the new is reflected in the University's buildings. While new structures accommodate growth, older buildings are adapted for new uses and it is these that are looked on with most affection by the city.

On Brownlow Hill is the Victoria Building, of 1887-92, by Alfred Waterhouse, designed to house the original University College before it became the University of Liverpool. Of red brick and terracotta, it is typical Waterhouse Gothic - romantic, turreted, imposing, its tall clocktower a local landmark. In striking contrast, a little further south, is Abercromby Square, a relic of Georgian Liverpool at its most elegant.

Wartime bombing and subsequent redevelopment took their toll on Liverpool's building stock but, at last, the city's precious architectural heritage is becoming much more widely appreciated and highly valued. So too is the city's amazing history and the contribution of those countless thousands who flocked to her shores, from all over Britain and the rest of the world. For example, in Liverpool can be found Europe's oldest Chinese community, still flourishing, rich in culture and much sought out by visitors and locals alike.

Liverpool has also suffered hard and long from economic recession following the swing away from the American market and the reduction of sea-trade in general but enterprises such as Wavertree Technology Park are creating the opportunities for growth. The redevelopment of Speke Airport and the success in attracting Freeport status are further examples of the city looking to the future.

The imagination with which the City Council and Merseyside Development Corporation have promoted tourism has also borne fruit. The Albert Dock is one of Britain's top three attractions with some six million visitors a year at the last count and rising.

The bold strategy of restoring Liverpool's historic docks and historic buildings is transforming the city for

the better. In the space of this short book, it has been possible to celebrate only a small selection of the many beautiful buildings and noteworthy developments that deserve attention. Nevertheless, they serve to convey the changing face of this remarkable city of Liverpool and to show, in some measure, the rich architectural and cultural heritage that we hold in trust.

(Above) Liverpool has the oldest Chinese community in Europe
(Left) A converted church, now Great George's Art Project, in the centre of Chinatown